Great Teachers Make school Bearable

Paintings by
Heidi Satterberg

HARVEST HOUSE PUBLISHERS

EUGENE, OREGON

Great Teachers Make School Bearable

Text Copyright © 2004 by Harvest House Publishers
Published by Harvest House Publishers
Eugene, Oregon 97402
www.harvesthousepublishers.com

ISBN 0-7369-1237-1

Artwork designs and original verse by Heidi Satterberg are reproduced under license from © Arts Uniq' ®, Inc., Cookeville, TN and may not be reproduced without permission. For more information regarding art prints featured in this book, please contact:

Arts Uniq'
P.O. Box 3085
Cookeville, TN 38502
1.800.223.5020

Design and production by Garborg Design Works, Minneapolis, Minnesota

Unless otherwise indicated, Scripture quotations are taken from the Holy Bible, New International Version®, Copyright © 1973, 1978, 1984 by the International Bible Society. Used by permission of Zondervan Publishing House. Scripture quotations marked KJV are from the King James Version.

Harvest House Publishers has made every effort to trace the ownership of all poems and quotes. In the event of a question arising from the use of a poem or quote, we regret any error made and will be pleased to make the necessary correction in future editions of this book.

Printed in Hong Kong

04 05 06 07 08 09 10 11 /NG/ 10 9 8 7 6 5 4 3 2 1

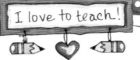

I love to teach!

Presented to:

_____

From:

_____

Because you make school bearable!

No bubble is so iridescent or floats longer
than that blown by the successful teacher.

SIR WILLIAM OSLER

is never any fuss.

Getting to and from my school

All I do is climb aboard

SCHOOL BUS

Heidi Satterberg©

a great big yellow bus.

the possibilities
for tomorrow are
usually beyond our
expectations.

AUTHOR UNKNOWN

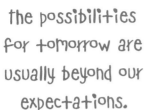

The dream begins with a teacher who
believes in you, who tugs and pushes and
leads you to the next plateau, sometimes
poking you with a sharp stick called "truth."

DAN RATHER

A heavy, copper-coloured beam of light came in at the west window, gilding the outlines of the children's heads with red gold, and falling on the wall opposite in a rich, ruddy illumination. Ursula, however, was scarcely conscious of it. She was busy, the end of the day was here, the work went on as a peaceful tide that is at flood, hushed to retire.

This day had gone by like so many more, in an activity that was like a trance. At the end there was a little haste, to finish what was in hand. She was pressing the children with questions, so that they should know all they were to know, by the time the gong went. She stood in shadow in front of the class, with catkins in her hand, and she leaned towards the children, absorbed in the passion of instruction.

D.H. LAWRENCE

Everyone who remembers his own educational experience remembers teachers, not methods and techniques. the teacher is the kingpin of the educational experience.

SIDNEY HOOK

Teach me your way, O LORD, and I will walk in your truth; give me an undivided heart, that I may fear your name.

THE BOOK OF PSALMS

In the new teacher she found another true and helpful friend. Miss Stacy was a bright, sympathetic young woman with the happy gift of winning and holding the affections of her pupils and bringing out the best that was in them mentally and morally. Anne expanded like a flower under this wholesome influence and carried home to the admiring Matthew and the critical Marilla glowing accounts of schoolwork and aims.

L.M. MONTGOMERY
Anne of Green Gables

Outside the principal's office door

We wait like little birds.

Then we're greeted with a smile,

and given encouraging words.

Principal

IN

Heidi Satterberg ©

To laugh often and much; to win the respect of intelligent people and the affection of children; to earn the appreciation of honest critics and endure the betrayal of false friends; to appreciate beauty, to find the best in others; to leave the world a bit better, whether by a healthy child, a garden patch, or a redeemed social condition. To know even one life has breathed easier because you have lived; this is to have succeeded.

RALPH WALDO EMERSON

The joy that you give to others

Each time we meet, you always have
Some word of praise that makes me glad.
You see some hidden, struggling trait,
Encourage it and make it great.
My day takes on a brand-new zest;
Your gift of praising brings my best,
Revives my spirit, flings it high;
For God loves praise, and so do I.

AUTHOR UNKNOWN

is the joy that comes back to you.

JOHN GREENLEAF WHITTIER

skill and training play a part;

Education is essential,

but to be a gifted teacher,

you must share it from your heart.

Heidi Satterberg ©

The man who can make hard things easy is the educator.

RALPH WALDO EMERSON

the gift of teaching is a peculiar talent and implies a need and a craving in the teacher himself.

JOHN JAY CHAPMAN

I am thankful you've spurred me on to grateful living, for people who are grateful are driven to help others just as they have been helped themselves.

AUTHOR UNKNOWN

Nan went to school early that afternoon, and as soon as she had left Bert and the two younger twins, she marched bravely to Mr. Tetlow's office and knocked on the door.

"Come in," said the principal, who was at his desk looking over some school reports.

"If you please, Mr. Tetlow, I came to see you about my brother, Bert Bobbsey," began Nan.

Mr. Tetlow looked at her kindly, for he half expected what was coming.

"What is it, Nan?" he asked.

"I—I—oh, Mr. Tetlow, won't you please let Bert off this time? He only did it because Danny said such things about me; said I was afraid of the ghost, and made all the boys call out that we had ghosts at our house. I—I—think, somehow, that I ought to be punished if he is."

There, it was out, and Nan felt the better for it. Her deep brown eyes looked squarely into the eyes of the principal.

In spite of himself Mr. Tetlow was compelled to smile. He knew something of how the Bobbsey twins were devoted to each other.

LAURA LEE
The Bobbsey Twins

Teaching is not just a job. It is a human service, and it must be thought of as a mission.

DR. RALPH TYLER

the function of education is to teach one to think intensively and to think critically. Intelligence plus character—that is the goal of true education.

MARTIN LUTHER KING, JR.

and science and music and art...

Reading, writing and arithmetic

one, alone, may teach all these –

thank goodness they're really smart.

If you plan for a decade, plant a tree. If you plan for a century, teach the children.

AUTHOR UNKNOWN

The important thing is not to stop questioning. Curiosity has its own reason for existing. One cannot help but be in awe when he contemplates the mysteries of eternity, of life, of the marvelous structure of reality. It is enough if one tries merely to comprehend a little of the mystery everyday. Never lose a holy curiosity.

ALBERT EINSTEIN

Give a little love to a child, and you get a great deal back.

JOHN RUSKIN

I ♥ KIDS

English has its "do's and don'ts"
that we musn't abuse or taint.
So please pass on this gentle hint:
There's no such word as "ain't."
I ain't saw nobody here.
I didn't see anybody here.
poems
literature
dictionary
Engl
TOM SAWYER
Fairy Tales
Shakespeare
DICTIONARY
GRAMMAR
SPELLING
POEMS
Little House
HeidiSatterberg©

Homework due!

A+

Spelling Test

dictionary
principal
experiment
school
library

to be successful, the first thing to do is fall in love with your work.

MARY LAURETTA

Education is the movement from darkness to light.

ALLAN BLOOM

TEACHER

"I wish you wouldn't talk against Miss Maxwell to me," said Rebecca hotly. "You know how I feel."

"I know; but I can't understand how you can abide her."

"I not only abide, I love her!" exclaimed Rebecca. "I wouldn't let the sun shine too hot on her, or the wind blow too cold. I'd like to put a marble platform in her class-room and have her sit in a velvet chair behind a golden table!"

KATE DOUGLAS WIGGIN
Rebecca of Sunnybrook Farm

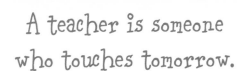

A teacher is someone who touches tomorrow.

JAN MILLER GIRANDO

Show me your ways, O LORD, teach me your paths; guide me in your truth and teach me, for you are God my Savior, and my hope is in you all day long.

THE BOOK OF PSALMS

the aim of education is the knowledge not of facts but of values.

DEAN WILLIAM RALPH INGE

There are two things we must give children:
The first one is roots, the other, wings.

AUTHOR UNKNOWN

the good life is
inspired by love and
guided by knowledge.

BERTRAND RUSSELL

What makes leadership is the ability to get
people to do what they don't want to do and like it.

HARRY TRUMAN

History's more than names and dates
on page after page we read.
It's real-life stories of women and men
who've changed our world indeed.
British law of 1765 - Stamp Act
protested against
"taxation without
a Party
PRESIDENTS
ANCIENT HISTORY
MEDIEVEL HISTORY
MODERN HISTORY
COLONIAL LIFE
AMERICAN HISTORY
WORLD HISTORY
CONSTITUTION
WWI
1783-Claims & Territories of 13 Original
Colonies.
Betsy Ross
1752-1836
legend says she made our first flag.
Heidi Satterberg ©

We think of the effective teachers we have had over the years with a sense of recognition, but those who have touched our humanity we remember with a deep sense of gratitude.

AUTHOR UNKNOWN

Give instruction to a wise man, and he will be yet wiser: teach a just man, and he will increase in learning.

THE BOOK OF PROVERBS (KJV)

How and Why

Still as children ask why
Adults gaze upon the sky.

Still, as children, grownups seek
Reason for the comet's streak;

Still to sages baffling are
Sun and planet, moon and star.

On a garden's tiny space
Miracles are taking place.

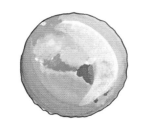

And as children, Age explores
God's bewildering out-of-doors.

Questioning, till the day they die,
Life's great mystery—how and why?

EDGAR GUEST

To teach is to learn twice.

JOSEPH JOUBERT

"**M**rs. Allan is perfectly lovely," she announced one Sunday afternoon. "She's taken our class and she's a splendid teacher. She said right away she didn't think it was fair for the teacher to ask all the questions, and you know, Marilla, that is exactly what I've always thought. She said we could ask her any question we liked and I asked ever so many."

L.M. MONTGOMERY
Anne of Green Gables

29

For good teaching rests neither in accumulating a shelfful of knowledge nor in developing a repertoire of skills. In the end, good teaching lies in a willingness to attend and care for what happens in our students, ourselves, and the space between us. Good teaching is a certain kind of stance, I think. It is a stance of receptivity, of attunement, of listening.

LAURENT DALOZ

I touch the future.
I teach.

CHRISTA MCAULIFFE

I'm curious about so many things, and there's more I want to discover about germs and stars and electricity and how chameleons change their color.

Heidi Satterberg ©

Teaching is the perpetual end and office of all things. Teaching, instruction is the main design that shines through the sky and earth.

RALPH WALDO EMERSON

Let my teaching fall like rain
and my words descend like dew,
like showers on new grass,
like abundant rain on tender plants.

THE BOOK OF DEUTERONOMY

It is by teaching that we teach ourselves, by relating that we observe, by affirming that we examine, by showing that we look, by writing that we think, by pumping that we draw water into the well.

HENRI-FRÉDÉRIC AMIEL

and continents we will probe;

Countries, mountains, rivers and seas,

to the north, east, south and west,

around and 'round the globe.

Geography
Oceans and Seas
MOUNTAINS

WORLD ATLAS

Heidi Satterberg ©

Reading Writing Arithmetic Science History

W hat office is there which involves more responsibility, which requires more qualifications, and which ought, therefore, to be more honourable, than that of teaching?

HARRIET MARTINEAU

Teaching is an instinctual art,
mindful of potential,
craving of realizations,
a pausing, seamless process.

A. BARTLETT GIAMATTI

Geography
Oceans and Seas
MOUNTAINS

Teacher praised him all she honestly could, and corrected his many blunders so quietly that he soon ceased to be a deep, distressful red during recitation, and tugged away so manfully that no one could help respecting him for his efforts, and trying to make light of his failures.

LOUISA MAY ALCOTT
Under the Lilacs

It has about all you need

A library is a place of adventure.

to go anywhere or do anything—

Read! Read! Read!

Heidi Satterberg ©

just open a book and read.

You can work miracles by having faith in others. To get the best out of people, choose to think and believe the best about them.

BOB MOAWAD

When I approach a child, he inspires in me two sentiments: tenderness for what he is, and respect for what he may become.

LOUIS PASTEUR

I'm never going to be a movie star. But then, in all probability, Liz taylor is never going to teach first and second grade.

MARY J. WILSON

☆ TEACHER ☆

Life is amazing—and the teacher had better prepare himself to be a medium for that amazement.

EDWARD BLISHEN

to each we give our all.

We learn the rules of sports and games,

But for health and safety's sake,

make sure you dodge that ball.

GYMNASIUM RULES
1. Play fair
2. Return balls
3. ...

Soccer

Heidi Satterberg ©

At the School Exercises

The fathers and the mothers on a certain happy day
Are called to watch their children in a pretty little play;
And the tired old faces glisten with the glory of a smile
For everything the youngsters do seems very much worthwhile.
The cares are all forgotten and their hearts with rapture beat
As the little sons and daughters dance about on nimble feet.

On the day of graduation weary eyes aglow with pride,
Every sign of disappointment bravely seem to put aside.
One would never guess to see them all the labor of the weeks
To teach that boy the verses which he now so proudly speaks.
In that hour of young achievement triumph hides each fault and scar,
And the fathers and the mothers of their cares forgetful are.

EDGAR GUEST

RED

41

Those having torches will

We call a child's mind "small" simply by habit; perhaps it is larger than ours, for it can take in almost anything without effort.

CHRISTOPHER MORLEY

Even if your days in the classroom are over, your days as a teacher will never end.

VICKI CARUANA

pass them on to others.

PLATO

Every child is born with a great capacity for knowledge…
The purpose of the teacher is to "draw out," not "cram
in." We must create interest in the heart and mind of the
child that will make him reach out and take hold upon
things he is taught.

HENRIETTA MEARS

A teacher affects
eternity; he can
never tell where his
influence stops.

HENRY ADAMS

Delightful task! to rear the tender thought,
to teach the young idea how to shoot,
to pour the fresh instruction o'er the mind,
to breathe the enlivening spirit and to fix
the generous purpose in the glowing breast!

JAMES THOMSON

44

I dream of traveling far away,
so now I find it's time
to learn the local language since
I'm not that good at mime.
FRANCE
MEXICO
GERMANY
JAPAN
ITALY
¡Buenos Di'as Clase!
SPANISH I
SPANISH II
NORWEGIAN
SWEDISH
ITALIAN
JAPANESE
SILENCE is not GOLDEN!
FRENCH I
FRENCH II
GERMAN
ATLAS
LATIN
CHINESE
Heidi Satterberg©

Before we leave, I hand my professor a present, a tan briefcase with his initials on the front. I bought this the day before at a shopping mall. I didn't want to forget him. Maybe I didn't want him to forget me.

"Mitch, you're one of the good ones," he says, admiring the briefcase. Then he hugs me, I feel his thin arms around my back. I am taller than he is, and when he holds me, I feel awkward, older, as if I were the parent and he were the child.

He asks if I will stay in touch, and without hesitation I say, "Of course."

When he steps back, I see that he is crying.

MITCH ALBOM
Tuesdays with Morrie

My heart is singing for joy this morning. A miracle has happened! the light of understanding has shone upon my little pupil's mind, and behold, all things are changed!

ANNE SULLIVAN

Those who educate children well are more to be honored than parents, for these only gave life, those the art of living well.

ARISTOTLE

FLAGS
by Justin

47

When a choir, a band or orchestra
plays music with a beat,
it stirs my heart and soul within...

and makes me tap my feet.

To sing with the teacher was a joy, but to hear the teacher sing to the accompaniment of her guitar was the supreme of bliss. It was not only an hour of pleasure to the pupils, but an hour of training as well.

RALPH CONNOR
The Doctor

Life is not measured by the number of breaths we take, but by the moments that take our breath away.

AUTHOR UNKNOWN

49

Teachers are the reason why airplanes fly, computers program, ballets are danced, novels are written, cancers researched, lawsuits won, skyscrapers built, and "art" decorates refrigerator doors. Life's biggest, boldest, brightest ideas—life's honors, achievements, and accomplishments—occur because somewhere, sometime, someone touched our lives—and it all began with a teacher.

AUTHOR UNKNOWN

to sculpt or paint a scene.

In art we're inspired to draw a face,

Yet it never hurts to know

that yellow and blue make green.

yellow + blue = green   red + yellow = orange

Heidi Satterberg ©

It is the supreme art of the teacher to awaken joy in creative expression and knowledge.

ALBERT EINSTEIN

the beautiful thing about learning is nobody can take it away from you.

B.B. KING

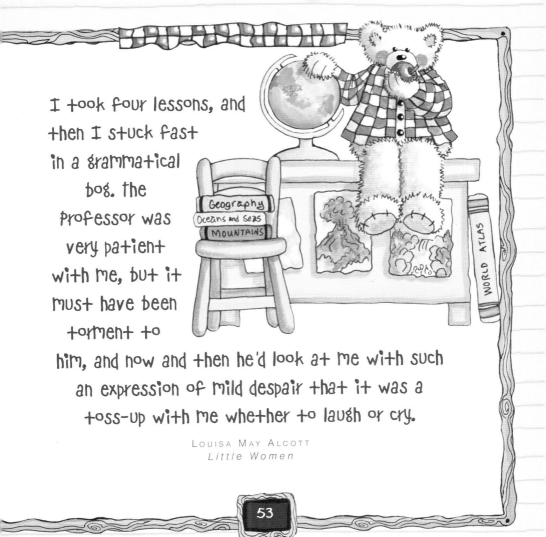

I took four lessons, and then I stuck fast in a grammatical bog. the professor was very patient with me, but it must have been torment to him, and now and then he'd look at me with such an expression of mild despair that it was a toss-up with me whether to laugh or cry.

LOUISA MAY ALCOTT
Little Women

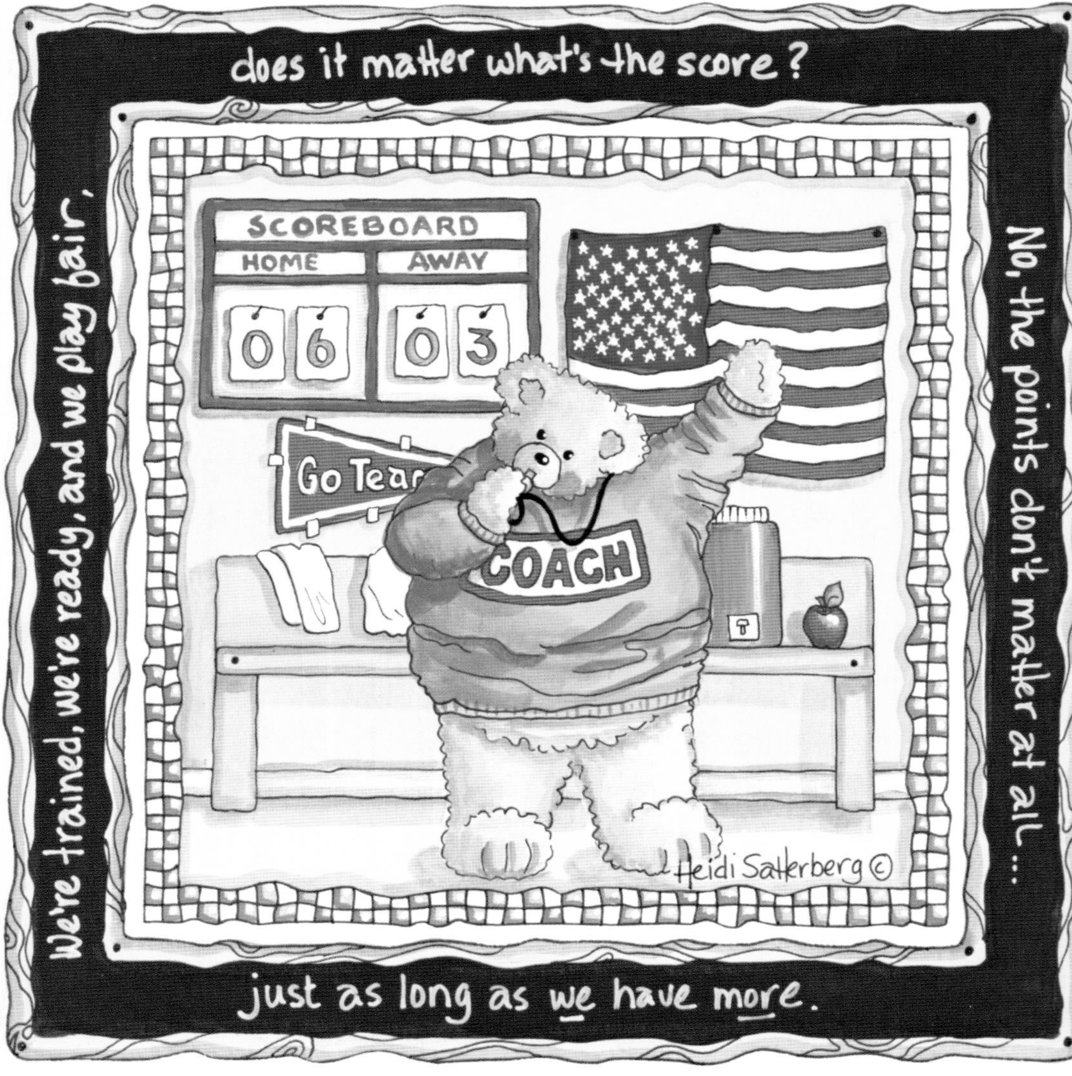
We're trained, we're ready, and we play fair,
does it matter what's the score?
No, the points don't matter at all...
just as long as we have more.
SCOREBOARD
HOME
AWAY
06
03
COACH
Heidi Satterberg ©

One of the most important things we adults can do for young children is to model the kind of person we would like them to be.

CAROL B. HILLMAN

A teacher must believe in the value and interest of his subject as a doctor believes in health.

GILBERT HIGHET

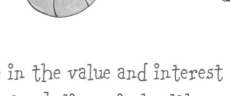

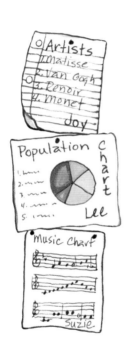

If I were asked what single qualification was necessary for one who has the care of children, I should say patience— patience with their tempers, patience with their understandings, with their progress— patience to go over first principles again and again; steadily to add a little every day; never to be irritated by willful or accidental hindrance.

FRANCIS DE S. FENELON

I shall pass through this world, but once.
Any good therefore that I can do,
Or any kindness that I can show to any human being,
Let me do it now. Let me not defer or neglect it,
For I shall never pass this way again.

MAHATMA GHANDI

God bless America

Teachers are expected to reach unattainable goals with inadequate tools. The miracle is that at times they accomplish this impossible task.

HAIM G. GINOT

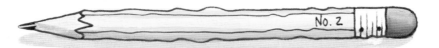

No. 2

A teacher knows that if he builds with love and truth, what he builds will last forever.

JOHN W. SCHLATTER

for generations yet to be.

Let's keep our patriotic spirit strong

May God continue to bless this land

I pledge allegiance to the Flag of the United States of America and to the Republic for which it stands, one Nation under God, indivisible, with liberty and justice for all.

United States

U.S.A.

God bless America

Heidi Satterberg ©

and keep it forever free.

'tis education forms the common mind. just as the twig is bent, the tree's inclin'd.

ALEXANDER POPE

Read! Read! Read!

Education is not filling a bucket, but lighting a fire.

WILLIAM YEATS

If a doctor, lawyer, or dentist had 40 people in his office at one time, all of whom had different needs, and some of whom didn't want to be there and were causing trouble, and the doctor, lawyer, or dentist, without assistance, had to treat them all with professional excellence for nine months, then he might have some conception of the classroom teacher's job.

Donald D. Quinn

While teachers have an important role, there are others if you look.

Some keep us clean, efficient and fed as they sweep, or type or cook.

Heidi Satterberg ©

A teacher is someone who sees each child as a unique person and encourages individual talents and strengths. A teacher looks beyond each child's face and sees inside their souls. A teacher is someone with a special touch and a ready smile who takes the time to listen to both sides and always tries to be fair. A teacher has a caring heart that respects and understands. A teacher is someone who can look past disruption and rebellion, and recognize hurt and pain. A teacher teaches the entire child and helps to build confidence and raise self-esteem. A teacher makes a difference in each child's life and affects each family and the future of us all.

BARBARA CAGE

63

the art of teaching is the art of assisting discovery.

MARK VAN DOREN